Like Zeros, Like Pearls

ALSO BY LOLA HASKINS

*Homelight**
Asylum: Improvisations on John Clare
How Small, Confronting Morning
The Grace to Leave
Fifteen Florida Cemeteries: Strange Tales Unearthed
Still, the Mountain
Not Feathers Yet: A Beginner's Guide to the Poetic Life
Solutions Beginning with A
Desire Lines: New and Selected Poems
The Rim Benders
Extranjera
A Lifetime from Any Land We Knew
Visions of Florida
Hunger
Forty-Four Ambitions for the Piano
Castings
Across Her Broad Lap Something Wonderful
Planting the Children

*From Charlotte Lit Press

Like Zeros, Like Pearls

Lola Haskins

CHARLOTTELIT
P R E S S

Charlotte Center for Literary Arts, Inc.
Charlotte, North Carolina
charlottelit.org

Copyright © 2025 by Lola Haskins
All rights reserved

ISBN: 978-1-960558-10-7

Library of Congress Control Number: 2025930369

Cover design and author photo by Charles Brown
Cover illustration by Yaohang Zhuang
Interior illustrations by Joon Thomas

Charlotte Lit Press
Charlotte Center for Literary Arts, Inc.
PO Box 18607, Charlotte, NC 28218
charlottelit.org/press

PROUD MEMBER
[clmp]
COMMUNITY OF LITERARY MAGAZINES & PRESSES
WWW.CLMP.ORG

The fourteenth Dalai Lama, when asked what he thought was the most important thing you can teach your children, replied "Teach them to love the insects."

Contents

Preface
    Point of Beginning   ix

One
    Dirt Road   3
    A Loaf of Bread   4
    First Instar   5
    Fire Ants   6
    Surgery   8
    Inside my right ear   9
    A Sting On My Ankle   10
    After the Picnic   11
    Mason Bee   12
    Incantation for a Dead Bee   13
    The Queens of Psithyrus   14
    The Consequence of Man's Disrespect for the Natural World, Expressed as the Sting of a Certain Wasp   16
    Confession   17

Two
    Field Notes   21
    Dominion   23
    Butterflies   24
    In Memoriam   25
    Poem Ending with an Image from *The Mustard Seed Garden Manual of Painting* (1782)   28
    The Great Peacock   29
    The Coleopterist's Dream   30
    In the Mountains of New Guinea   31

A Short History of Iridescence	32
Navigating Night	33
Periodicity	34
Lantern Bug	35
Fireflies, East of Asheville	36
Sphingid Moth, Thailand	39

Three

Water Striders	43
Odonata	45
Damselfly	46
Dragon, Skimming Over the Creek	47
Shell	48
The Spirituality of Cicadas	50
European Stag Beetle	51
Beetles	52
Glow Worm's Dinner	53
Imago: Portrait of a Young Poet	54
Four Small Portraits	55
Ladybug	57
Two Stick Insects	58
Waltz	61
The Dead Mouse	62
Sybarites	63
The Dew-Tasters	64

Acknowledgments	69
A Modest Bibliography	71
About the Author	73

Preface

Dear Reader,

For most of my life, aside from childhood entertainments like ant farms and butterfly spectating, the only time I noticed insects was when they called attention to themselves by being beautifully marked or by attacking me. But one day about fifteen years ago, I walked out of my house and suddenly realized that ignoring whole worlds wasn't okay, so I set out to learn everything I could about what was happening in the air around me and in the ground under my feet. I had no idea at the time what astonishing stories I'd find, and how most things that looked simple at first, would turn out not to be. Butterflies and fire ants are perfect examples of this. Butterflies—those epitomes of beauty—will feed on road kill or puddles of urine and excrement if those are what's on offer. And listen to this! Fire ants, who are so small you may not notice them until they bite, mate 400 feet above the ground, after which the males disappear; you'd think the females eat them but no one has seen them do this. And then, when a female hits the ground, the first thing she does—even before she seeks shelter—is tear off her own wings (which like dancers' costumes are designed to come off easily). One reason is that since she'll fly only once, they're superfluous after she mates, but the less obvious reason—and a perfect metaphor for the cost of motherhood—is that she does it so her wing-muscles can be converted to food to feed the clutches of eggs she'll spend the rest of her life laying.

Because I live in a university town, I began by interviewing faculty members about their areas of interest. Unfortunately, this was so long ago that I can't find their names any more—but I can assure you they were thrilling to talk to, and that I made good use of what they told me. After that, I went to the science library and checked out the books they recommended, which proved yet again that there are more things on heaven and earth than I'd had any idea of. I was especially surprised to see how many beetles, who represent a quarter of all living creatures, are so beautifully patterned that, along with snakes, tree bark, flowers, and ripples on water, they make you wonder why fabric designers bother. I also read a number of books that non-scientist friends suggested, the most useful of which were written by the amateur naturalist Henri Fabre. I put my favorites of those books in the back of this one in case you want to know more.

When the manuscript rose to the top of my submissions pile, I wanted to accomplish two things before it was published—to be sure the stories it tells were accurate and to freshen it for myself by adding to it. At this point, several young entomologists volunteered to help me, so I sent each of them my most recent effort and what I got back left me newly energized—first, because to my surprise all of them related to it, second, because they straightened me out on facts and formats that weren't professionally correct, and third because they had such stellar ideas for more stories.

Having said all that, I want to explain something. At first, I thought my quest was to learn as much as I could about the way insects live their lives but it didn't take long for me to realize that the only way to make what I was learning three-dimensional was to include the ways we humans relate to them. That's the point of the title. It started out as a straightforward description of insect eggs on grass but ended up a metaphor for our bifurcated attitude towards bugs. If they do things that benefit us, like pollinate, they are pearls and within our limits, we take care of them. If they don't, they are zeros and depending on how much trouble they cause us, either we ignore them or we kill them.

I think you'll notice in the course of these stories that insects conduct themselves not as differently from us as you might have thought. If you're a scientist, you'll stick to the facts—and you should—but if you aren't, and you go where the facts take you, in the associational way we (I, anyway) read poems, that's legitimate too. And one more thing—Besides not soft-pedalling the downside of our species, I've tried to be honest about the inconsistent way we as individuals, unless we're the Dalai Lama, behave. Take me. Most of the time I open my door and fan intruders outside or if the intruders are with roaches, trap them in a jar and shake them one by one into the hedge. But I've also found myself for no justifiable reason swatting a fly or crushing a tiny runner I notice only because it contrasts with the wall it's crossing. Personal slips like mine may be forgivable, or not. But when we consistently kill our zeros by spraying them with poison or by putting out lethal snacks—which is easier because we don't have to watch—and especially when we manipulate them genetically so we can eliminate whole populations at once, it's different, because those are actions whose consequences we can't predict so, and not for the first time, we may be changing forever not just their viability but our own.

Lola Haskins
Gainesville, Florida

Point of Beginning

I slap the fly that pauses on the window.

And as its small life falls to the sill

I realize how much older that fly

was than the glass, than any glass.

One

Dirt Road

A dung beetle pushes

its round work

over a mountain thrown

up by a passing car.

A Loaf of Bread

A trail of ants

each carrying a single crumb

disappears

into an o

the shape of one boy's mouth

whistling to another.

First Instar

Stagmomantis floridensis

A mantis lifts its sickle moons

to bless the woman

on the bed and

the new-to-the-air child

who has just discovered her breast.

Fire Ants

Solinopsis invicta

1. The Speck

finds its mate

in a thin cirrus of other specks

four hundred feet

above the earth.

Afterwards, the female

tears off her wings.

Kick a mound

and specks

startle in all directions

like handfuls

of tiny lights.

2. The Beauty of Ants

The night the field

became a lake,

we leaned from

our canoes and

torched each

black lace raft

until,

as if it were

flowering,

the water flamed.

Surgery

Camponotus Floridanus

A carpenter ant will lick

its neighbor's wounded

leg to the shoulder then

bite it off. Amputation

may take fifteen minutes

to complete, and typically

involves multiple surgeons.

We operate too. When one

of our workers falls behind,

we let him go and get another.

Inside my right ear

a mosquito whines, not

like something flying

but like an old woman

tied to a chair

who keens

without knowing she does.

A Sting On My Ankle

I'm sorry, I tell the grass.

I didn't mean to startle you.

After the Picnic

A pale ring appears

around the bite

like the glowing

aureole a full moon

casts on a clearing

as an alien ship

floats slowly down.

Mason Bee

Osmia lignaria

Mason bees live solitarily. Some subspecies have unusual habits, such as lining their nest cavities with flower petals.

Like a religious

you stack your eggs in reeds

and seal each chamber

with a dome of clay.

An indian in a hat

stands in the wind;

his lips are pressed to

a bamboo flute.

He is calling the hums

inside his heart.

He is calling his bees.

Incantation for a Dead Bee

I will wrap you in a leaf
and cup my hands

over you.
Inside your red dome

you are powerful.
Where the light comes

between my fingers
you are powerful.

Flower-dust on your legs
you are powerful.

I will lay you into
the earth, bee.

Under your small mound
you are powerful.

I am nothing, bee,
next to you.

The Queens of Psithyrus

Bomba psithyrus

visit flowers frequented by

a foreign colony long enough

to assume its odor, so that

when they penetrate it, no

alarm will be raised. Once

inside, they'll stab its queen

and destroy her eggs and

larvae. After that, the colony's

workers will feed both their

new queen and the eggs she's

laid, peacefully if they're fooled,

but if not, by violence. One

could argue that because

these queens birth no workers

of their own, their predations

are necessary. On the other

hand, since as soon as they

begin to rule, they take

everything from their subjects

and contribute nothing in return

but offspring like themselves,

perhaps they're not. Think

cruelty. Think greed.

Think the rise of empires.

Think their inevitable fall.

The Consequence of Man's Disrespect for the Natural World, Expressed as the Sting of a Certain Wasp

You grow very sleepy.

Then, like a breached ship

on a darkening sea,

you slip out of sight.

Confession

You crossed my white wall.

I crushed you without

a thought. Then

I washed my hands.

Two

Field Notes

1

Myrmecia sanguinea (Wheeler, 1916)

Thousands, perhaps hundreds of thousands lit on the black-thorn bushes atop Mount Armour. Then struggling balls of males formed around each mating pair until one by one the balls collapsed, and as their scurrying contents rose up the sides of my boots, even I, a man of science, was afraid.

2

Myrmecia rubra (Farron-White, 1876)

He saw clouds of ants gyrating in the air above a small beech tree near Stonehenge, their paths and intersects like the red dodder that lays its tiny blossoms over gorse. Then the ants spiraled upwards like a tree gone to flame and when his cheeks turned hot enough, he joined the others, dancing around the stones

3

Ants who enslave other ants eventually become incapable of doing anything but fighting and preening and would, if not for the work of their prisoners, starve. E.O. Wilson says there is no conclusion to be drawn from this.

4

Certain beetles introduce themselves to passing ants by raising their abdomens to be licked-- rather like a dog offering his bottom to another dog-- and releasing a tranquilizing ooze. Then, since the pheromones they emit remind the potential host of his own, they are ceremoniously transported into that worthy's chambers and for the rest of their lives, fed whenever they tap a passing worker with an antenna and present their mouths. Some of these freeloading beetles even change their quarters in the winter. Bert Holldobler, writing in *Scientific American*, remains carefully in the realm of insects.

Dominion

In 1578, Mark Scaliot fashioned a padlock from eleven pieces of iron, steel and brass, attached it to a gold chain, and slipped it over the neck of a flea. No one thought to emulate him until 250 years later, when flea circuses became widely popular.

Some ringmasters sort their prisoners into two groups then outfit each with a harness, hitched to a cart if a flea is a runner, a ball if it jumps. Others glue musical instruments to their charges' thoraxes, then glue their legs to the floor of their enclosure and apply shocks from underneath.

Since fleas' back legs are very strong, their ever-more-desperate efforts to free themselves send their carts and balls careening in the first case, and their instruments oscillating with the apparent élan of tiny Dizzy Gillespies in the second, effects most people find highly entertaining.

Butterflies

In the long cage with its rows of pupae

a white peacock struggles from her casing and hangs,

drying. A watching five year old, entranced, leaves

his fingerprints on the glass.

*

Inside the museum, framed specimens line the walls

like innocents whom someone told,

open your arms wide. No, wider.

*

An entomologist parses the markings of a wood nymph

pinned in a drawer. Her wings flutter a little,

sensing the open window.

*

In the screened garden, butterflies bright as saris perch

on glossy leaves, feed, folded, at laid-open fruit, wink

like iridescent stars among the flowers and streams.

I look at you. What have we ever done to deserve this?

In Memoriam

Papilio cresphontes

You appeared on
my front porch, not
a breath of flutter
in your beautiful wings:

a black sky lined
with stars, tipped in
blue orange yellow
stripes with black

between, like medals
awarded for great
bravery. When,
thinking you were

gone, I bent to
see you better and
your thin black feet
slid you away

so slowly I could

hardly tell they

moved, I knew

to leave you be.

In the morning you were

clinging to the screen,

so still I could have

drawn you square by

tiny square, and all day

every time I went in

or out, I whispered

the door into position

oblivious to the fact

that whether you

lived or died had

nothing to do with me.

The third morning,

I thought you flown

until I looked off

the edge of the porch

and saw your parted
wings, one moving,
the others still, and
where they had joined,

a commotion of ants,
as if your body had
been replaced by a
corsage of dark roses.

Then, slowly, solemnly,
your wings began
processing towards
a scatter of sand and

when I went out again
the path and porch
were bare and below
the earth the ants were

less hungry. Someday
I'll be a gift like that.

Poem Ending with an Image from *The Mustard Seed Garden Manual of Painting* (1782)

Pterophyllia camellifolia

Only after the twelfth instar are

the ears on her legs ready to listen

so only now when he calls her

across the dusk does she answer,

softly at first, then not. When they

are near enough, he climbs onto her

and for hours they move only

slightly, he to devour nearby leaves,

she, to reach underneath herself

to consume the jelly that clouds

his sperm. By dawn the male will

have flown, and his mate with

her camellia wings, but double rows

of eggs will glisten along the twigs

they've left, like zeros, like pearls.

The Great Peacock

*In the 19th century, Henri Fabre tried to discover the mechanism
by which peacock moths, who live only two days, attract mates.
He died, not knowing.*

She wears dark-red velvet

with an ermine collar.

A purple, white, and chestnut eye

adorns the skirt of each wing.

For two nights

myriad pale shapes

big as birds

flutter around her cage.

On the third,

we find her dead

in an empty room.

In our candlelit

single file

up the stairs,

we too are ghosts.

We too have no mouths.

The Coleopterist's Dream

On my love's back a turquoise river curved through hazard green. While he slept, I explored the trees along its banks, high above the black whirlpools. Sometimes the lanterns of other seekers lit my way. But to no avail, for in all my time with my beetle, I never found what I was looking for nor could I have told you what it was. One morning I woke and found him dead. It was only then I understood that he carried no color at all, and never had.

In the Mountains of New Guinea

Colydinae and certain Coleoptra cultivate on their shells blue-green algae, hepatica, mosses, lichens, fungi and the prothalli of opening ferns, forests in which diatoms feed. If will alone could make me small, I'd walk those lush wild heights only to feel under my footsoles, the fused elytra where psocids graze as I lurch invisibly over the clumps of moss that line my branch as it widens towards the trunk, like a river to the sea.

A Short History of Iridescence

The apparent colors of the scarab are illusions created by light passing through layers of wing scales offset like randomly dropped cards.

Ancient Egyptians would place a scarab made of schist or jade on a gold chain over the heart of a mummy, to speak for him when he reached the underworld.

*

Roman soldiers wore scarabs into battle as tokens of their masculinity.

*

For some early Christians, scarabs were symbolic of the Resurrection.

*

The *Physiologus*, a natural history written in the second century AD, describes the scarab as made of excrement, living in filth, and carrying the stench of heresy.

*

In medieval Europe, a scarab placed inside a chest was thought to fill it with riches.

*

A wise man or woman will understand that, depending on the light, each of these is true.

Navigating Night

African beetles can roll their balls

of dung in straight lines only if

they can see the Milky Way. Put

a lid over them, and they founder.

As do we, day by smoky day.

Periodicity

Apis mellifera

A queen arcs across the sky

pursued by a tail of drones.

One breaks his phallus

into her sting chamber,

falls backward, and dies.

This will happen five,

six, seven times. Once

Halley's comet passed

overhead, its living tail

abuzz. I will be

long gone before

it comes again.

Lantern Bug

Pyrops candelabria

Splashed across

the narrow netting

of your dark green wings,

an archipelago of suns.

No wonder the Nanti

think you glow.

No wonder their men

believe you

make them hard.

And why not,

here in the dripping forest

where no one can see

even into the close distance,

from which at night

the small cries come.

Fireflies, East of Asheville

Phausis reticula

Blue lights streak between
darkened trees, glow
on the leafy floor.

A long time ago soldiers
died here. They're back
tonight, searching for

their women, insects
all, but not. For what
can years and bodies

signify, compared to love?
Nothing, say the males
emitting their shines.

Nothing, say the females
who cannot fly but
generation on generation,

crawl and climb. If you

stand on the edge of

these woods at dusk

when the ghosts are out,

you're bound to see how

the men are so faithful

they don't even blink,

as their larval women,

who can be crushed

by any careless foot or paw,

creep glowing anyhow over

the leaves, some of which

are almost earth, then

curl onto bark, inch up,

and wait. And sometimes,

in a form they could

not have imagined

when they pinned up

their hair and wore skirts

so long they pooled at

their feet, they are found.

Sphingid Moth, Thailand

Rhagastis olivacea

An air engineer

lover of speed and shine

crouches in

the undergrowth

as Rhagastis, sleek

as any jet

in her slender brown sleeves

and pointed skirt

swing-hovers

towards

a nameless orchid's

throat and

suddenly the engineer

understands

that no matter

how many times

the metals he's sketched

may carry him

down a runway,

he will never once

feel this.

Three

Water Striders

Gerridae

seek a pond or river that has been silent a long time

and speed across its surface on dry bodies,

front legs poised for a struggling dragonfly or surfacing

larva which they suck empty, middle legs

powering ahead, back legs guiding. When their times come,

they signal each other by sending out ripples.

For this, they are sometimes called Jesus bugs. Also

because if their water falls too far,

they burrow into mud and wait, and in winter cold

crawl inside plant stems and wait

so when they resurrect we think they came from nowhere.

Some striders, though, live all their lives

in open sea. And what will these do when the sea crusts and the sky rains fire?

We put this to them as a koan, but like all masters they will not say.

Odonata

125,000,000 years ago tiny black needles
with wrap-around eyes hovered
above the grass

while huge green not-birds darted and
skimmed in the slurried air
over ponds

whole galaxies of lace-winged fliers
millions of years from names,
millions of years before

anything living would learn to read
stones. And yet on the toe
of my boot this morning

something minute perched.
O Dragonlet
O Handsome Clubtail

O Coppery Emerald
O Sprite
O Powdered Dancer vanishing against the blue

Damselfly

Argia moesta

You conceal yourself at eye level,

your transparent wings veined,

your abdomen shining green,

its slender stem tensed upward

and slightly swollen at the tip.

Shafts of light wash the leaves

around you, flood the slabs

of bark to which you cling,

the crevices between,

your wings, your six thin legs,

me, my jeans, my red jacket,

all one pattern.

Dragon, Skimming Over the Creek

Odonata Anisoptera

Electric blue! The color of

now what? A two year-old,

jumping up and down,

and pointing at the stage!

Shell

Magicicada septendecim

The cicada emerges

from her slit skin

as delicately

as someone stepping from

a bath

unfolds

the damp green appendages

that will let her fly

opens them

to the air.

Abandoned,

her husk

is pure light.

*

Any child can tell you

that what he balances

on his palm,

carefully, so as not

to let the wind steal it,

is all there is.

The Spirituality of Cicadas

The Ancient Chinese believed they were spirits, because they consumed only dew and by 4,000 years ago were placing their replicas on the tongues of the dead.

*

Two millennia later, "Slough Off the Cicada's Golden Shell" appeared in *Thirty-Six Stratagems,* along with "Kill with a Borrowed Knife" and "Befriend a Distant State While Attacking a Neighbor."

*

The Ancient Greeks believed they were humans transformed by the Gods and ate only air.

*

I believe that when my musician son is gone from here, he will teach himself their song.

European Stag Beetle

Lucanus cervus

Because you swarm when the sky
turns heavy, we call you thunderdoll
and kill you to protect our thatch,

then we snap your heads
and slip them in our pockets,
or give them to our wives

to dangle from their wrists,
or to our daughters to weave
into their braids. We powder

your bodies to use for love.
Though God's bells call
fervently as mating birds.

Though every Sunday
we rise from our beds
and answer them: Amen.

Beetles

One out of every four creatures on earth is a beetle.

God said: if they will be many, then let them be beautiful.

So in His *Book of Beetles*

he drew dark islands, and bearers of treasure,

and fires at the hearts of forests.

God said: and let the end of beauty be vanishment.

Into tropical green flecked with light.

Into the dotted throats of lilies.

Into red sand.

And when the moon bares her milk, said God,

let the few reverence the many.

In Japan, in a seventh century shrine:

nine thousand shimmering elytra

set in gold.

Glow Worm's Dinner

The lampyris covers a snail's foot

with bites until the snail

can no longer move.

A few more kisses liquefy

the flesh whose sweet

juice he sucks. Finally,

there remains only a shell

clinging to its grass stalk.

You asked me about love.

Imago: Portrait of a Young Poet

Chiloloba acuta

It's not her elytra,

glittery and hard,

but the second, delicate pair

of wings they conceal,

folded along artful veins,

that when it's time

will open and carry her.

Four Small Portraits

Dragonfly

Odonata aeshnidae

You were born breathing water.
Grown, you push your prey from the air
into the basket of your legs
o angel bright as grass
hovering above the red flowers.

Leafhopper

Hemiptera fulgoriodea

Your husk is white with
black scatters
pale yellow at the tip.
If I could take you home
I would hold you to my ear
and listen for the sea.

Cricket, Vietnam

Oecanthus fultoni

Snowy tree crickets
synchronize their songs
until leaf, branch, and core
are one repeating
tremble. When Yen
was asked
to define moonlight,
in pearl and dim blue
she painted this.

Katydid, Yucatán

*Meconmatina phrixa maya: The calls of this species are
inaudible to us.*

Deep in the tangled bosque
a bright yellow leaf
calls out, over and over again.

Sometimes, tesoro, when
it's very late and we're lying
in our hammock, every bone
in my heart feels you dream.

Ladybug

Cocinellida

Our Lady's Bird
wears a fine, red cloak.
And on it
seven spots:
seven sorrows
seven joys.

Our Lady's Bird
belongs
to her Lord
and to
the high clouds.

In the painting
Our Lady holds
her bird on
one white finger
and sings to it
what women have
always sung.

Two Stick Insects

Podocanthus typhoon

        Watercolour, Thomas Watling, Australia 1792-1797

Whoever named you

did not see you as you are:

elegant as a fine kimono

with your four understated wings

dark green against your dark red body.

The way it tapers to elongated pincers

is lovely enough to bring anyone's brush to tears.

I was certain I could render

your pleasures for all the world to see

but I have come to realize

that there is something in you

I cannot paint

and will never understand.

Phasmidae

> *The voracious appetites of Phasmidae create*
> *the gaps in tropical forests which allow the*
> *great trees to climax as they reach for the sun.*

Under a leaf, a twig rocks

from side to side as if

a breeze has found it.

A winged male

steadies her abdomen

and inserts himself.

When she is flown,

the abandoned leaf will

weep for her. But it need not,

for after she has buried

her eggs, she will return

and consume it.

As with us and our own

mysteries, Phasmidae were

never twigs, but they serve them.

A Field in Spring

In Japanese ink-painting, the mantis body stroke is used to render the point at which blades of grass widen.

The painter slashes mantises

across the page.   But when

he turns and walks away

it is not the field that remains.

It is his gestures in the air.

Waltz

The White-edged Sphex embraces a locust

who flutters her wings' red fans and

stretches her drowsy extremities.

When she stops moving

he pulls her between his legs,

and, clasping one of her antennae

in his mandibles,

glides over the dewy grass.

Such partnering! Will the locust

dream of the moment the Sphex

arrives at his burrow and slides

her down? Of the slow way

dark spreads over her

as he throws up dirt

like rain to seal her in?

The Dead Mouse

The burying beetles have

set my fur to quivering

as if I have just discovered

some tasty morsel in the grass.

As their heads and legs

nudge me from underneath

I sink into the soft sand

that shines almost gold.

And suddenly I believe

in them, priests

that they are

in their dust robes.

Sybarites

Ants pull baby mantises from their sheaths

as they leave the nest.

 A lizard half-shuts her eyes at the taste

on her slender tongue.

We call the empty boats beautiful

whose few survivors

scatter then disappear into

the wide leaves.

The Dew-Tasters

Drosophilia melanogaster

X was my grandfather, you say, and Y who supervised my post-doc my father. You recite your lineage with pride as if ideas were blood to be passed on. In your office you keep a pair of portraits, male and female, dated 1910, their wings and heads perfectly inked then tinted in yellows and soft grays by Z's own hand, royals to you, who lived a few days then were gone, generations of whom have flown and been forgotten since you and I made this date. And why should X not be your grandfather, or for that matter you my brother, for both our eyes shine as we approach the waiting lenses in your lab that smells of ether because what we each love is to look at very small things carefully.

*

On black-veined wings

she tries the air

The fine hairs

on her foot

find the papaya

sweet

She slides into it

egg egg egg

    *

Under the microscope

the ether has not

quite taken.

Teased upside down

she waves translucent

legs.

I edge her upright.

She struggles against

the brush.

I poke at her ovaries

I, voyeur,

so flushed.

*

Holding a cloth over

the bottle, he says:

Sometimes,

to see something clearly

you have to kill it.

*

I cup my hands around

the rubber guards

to focus a male

nudged to

to the center of the tile.

His transformed eyes

glow blue.

His pointed thorax

is a red smear.

The new colors float

against the dark,

beautiful as space dust.

What have we done?

Acknowledgments

Acumen: "Odonata"

Analog Science Fiction and Fact (Dell): "Field Notes"

Another Chicago Magazine: "Point of Beginning," "Dominion," "The Consequence of Man's Disrespect for the Natural World as Expressed in the Sting of a Certain Wasp," and "Beetles"

Crab Creek Review: "Confession"

Georgia Review: "The Dew-Tasters," "Cricket," and "Katydid"

Green Mountains Review: "Mason Bee," "Incantation for a Dead Bee," "Fire Ants," and "The Great Peacock"

I-70 Review: "Waltz" and "A Field in Spring"

Innisfree Poetry Journal: "In Memoriam," "East of Asheville, 2023," and " Queens of Psithyrus"

Iodine: "Dragonfly" and "Leafhopper"

Julebord: "Dragonfly"

Lake Effect: "Inside my Right Ear"

New Letters: "Water Striders" and "Magicicada septemdecim"

Salamander: "European Stag Beetle"

San Diego Poetry Annual 2016-17: "Butterflies" and "Two Stick Insects"

Smartish Pace: "Sybarites"

South Florida Review: "Sphingid Moth, Thailand"

Southern Review: "A Short History of Iridescence," "Glow Worm's Dinner," and "Imago"

The Scream Online: "The Coleopterist's Dream"

Thorny Locust: "Lantern Bug"

"Field Notes" was anthologized in T*he Heartbeat of the Universe, Poems from Asimov's Science Fiction and Analog Science Fiction and Fact, 2012-2022* (Interstellar Flight Press, 2024).

"A Field in Spring" was reprinted in *Cadence,* FSPA.

"Navigating Night" appeared in *Celestial Musings: Poems Inspired by the Night Sky* (Charles W. Brown Planetarium at Ball State University in Indiana, 2019).

"Field Notes" was nominated by *Analog* for the 2014 Rhysling Price for the year's best science poem.

"Two Stick Insects" was reprinted in *Serving House Journal.*

Heartfelt thanks to UF research scientist Al Holder for the interview-cum-lab-visit that led to "The Dewtasters," to entomologists Jon Elmquist, Anne Johnson and Tyler Jones for their comments on the manuscript and suggestions for new stories, to entomologist Codey Mathis for all of that and for editing help, , to Charles Brown for moral support and cover design, to Haoyang Zhuang for permission to use the cover painting, and to calligrapher Joon Thomas for his gift of the wandering insects that grace this book's insides.

A Modest Bibliography

Beckmann, Poul and Beckman, Ruth: *Living Jewels*

Buchmann, Stephen and Nabhan, Gary Paul: *The Forgotten Pollinators*

Danforth, Bryan, Minckley, Robert, and Neff, John: *The Solitary Bees: Biology, Evolution, Conservation*

Durin, Bernard: *Beetles and Other Insects*

Fabre, Jean-Henri: *Fabre's Book of Insects, The Social Life of the Insect World*, and many others

Holldobler, Bert and Wilson, E. O.: *Journey to the Ants*

Hubbell, Sue: *Broadsides from the Other Orders*

Wilson, E. O.: *The Insect Societies* and many others

Wilson, Joseph and Carril, Olivia Messinger: *The Bees in Your Backyard: A Guide to North America's Bees*

About the Author

Besides 14 books of poetry, Lola Haskins has published three of prose, including *Fifteen Florida Cemeteries: Strange Tales Unearthed* (University Press of Florida), *Not Feathers Yet: A Beginner's Guide to the Poetic Life* (University of Nebraska Press), and *Solutions Beginning with A* (Modernbook), a collection of fables about women illustrated by Maggie Taylor.

The past ten or fifteen years have seen ventures into the natural world, both in poetry and prose. Her poem "Prayer for the Everglades" ends the otherwise prose *The Book of the Everglades* (Milkweed), and another poem, "The View from Cedar Key," is one of two poems in *UnspOILed (Heart of the Earth)*, a book of citizens' responses to the Gulf, given to all state legislators prior to the Deepwater Horizon oil spill. *How Small, Confronting Morning* (Jacar) is set in the woods and on the waters of north-central Florida. She has also written an as-yet unpublished collection of personal essays beginning in Florida state parks, called *Wind, the Grass, and Us*.

Haskins particularly relishes collaboration, especially with musicians. She and cellist Ben Noyes created a CD of poems from *The Grace to Leave*. Composer Paul Richards (University of Florida Department of Music) has issued a two CD set of all forty-four of her ambitions for the piano for voice and piano. Composer Willis Bodine's settings for choir and hand bells of 11 of her nature poems concluded University of Floridas 2012 Choral Music Festival. She has also collaborated on a number of occasions with visual artists, most recently with collagist Derek Gores; and with dancers, most recently with choreographer Judy Skinner of Dance Alive! in "Land of La Chua," which premiered at UF's Performing Arts Center in Spring 2019. Two favorite past ventures with Dance Alive! involved playing the role of Mata Hari, using a script she wrote for a ballet of that title and a performance celebrating the opening of the American Art Wing of the Harn Museum in Gainesville, in which dancers enacted poems about four characters inspired by Cindy Sherman photographs. Among her favorite multimedia pieces was *Swan Song*, directed by Ani Collier and performed at the Hippodrome State Theater with seven dancers, an actor, and a violinist.